COUNTRY EXPLORERS

GREECE

Madeline Donaldson

Lerner Publications Company • Minneapolis

Lerner Publications Company
A division of Lerner Publishing Group, Inc.
241 First Avenue North
Minneapolis, MN 55401 U.S.A.

Website address: www.lernerbooks.com

Library of Congress Cataloging-in-Publication Data

Donaldson, Madeline.
    Greece / by Madeline Donaldson.
        p.   cm. — (Country explorers)
    Includes index.
    ISBN 978–1–58013–600–6 (lib. bdg. : alk. paper)
    1. Greece—Juvenile literature. I. Title.
DF717.D66 2009
949.6—dc22   2008014211

Manufactured in the United States of America
1 2 3 4 5 6 – PA – 14 13 12 11 10 09

Table of Contents

Welcome!

Wow! What a blast to travel through Greece. This country is in the southeastern corner of Europe. Albania and Macedonia are to the northwest. Bulgaria sits to the north. To the northeast is Turkey.

Greece

Ancient Names

Modern Greeks call their country Hellas. They call themselves Hellenes. These names date from thousands of years ago.

Ancient and modern buildings stand side by side in Athens, Greece's capital city.

MACEDONIA

BULGARIA

TURKEY

ALBANIA

THRACE

mountains

country's capital

Parthenon

M A C E D O N I A

VARDAR RIVER

Thessaloniki

GREECE

THESSALY

CORFU

EPIRUS

PENEUS RIVER

AEGEAN
SEA

N

EUBOEA

S P O R A D E S   I S L A N D S

MILES

0   25   75   75

0   25 50 75 100
KILOMETERS

GULF OF
PATRAS

ACHELOUS RIVER

PINDUS MOUNTAINS

BOEOTIA

EUBOEA

TURKEY

IONIAN
ISLANDS

GULF OF CORINTH

ATTICA

Patras

★ 🏛
Athens

PELOPONNESE

IONIAN
SEA

CYCLADES
ISLANDS

D O D E C A N E S E   I S L A N D S

RHODES

CRETE

MEDITERRANEAN SEA

Two Parts

Greece has two main parts—the mainland and many islands. The mainland of Greece touches the continent of Europe. This part makes up four-fifths of the country.

The city of Kavala is on mainland Greece. You can see the island of Thasos across the Aegean Sea.

Dozens of Greek islands dot the seas to the east, south, and west of the mainland. These islands make up the other one-fifth of Greece.

Map Whiz Quiz

Take a look at the map on page 5. A map is a drawing or chart of a place. Trace the outline of Greece on a sheet of paper. Don't forget the islands! See if you can find the Aegean Sea. Mark this part of your map with an *E* for east. How about Bulgaria? Mark this side with an *N* for north. With a green crayon, color in Greece. Color Albania, Macedonia, and Bulgaria yellow to show where they end and the Greek mainland begins. (Note: Macedonia is a region of Greece. But the same name is given to a separate country. Be sure you color them correctly!)

Greece has many islands. But people live on only about 160 of them. Many people live on the Greek island of Crete *(left)*.

Mainland Greece

Most of the mainland is rocky. The Pindus Mountains are in northwestern Greece. These mountains stretch southward until they reach the Gulfs of Patras and Corinth. These waterways divide a big peninsula from the rest of mainland Greece. The peninsula is called the Peloponnese. It has water on three sides.

Roads weave through the Pindus Mountains.

Mount Olympus is the highest spot in Greece. It rises 9,570 feet (2,917 meters) in Thessaly.

South central Greece has three regions. They are Boeotia, Attica, and Euboea. Thessaly is a region in north central Greece. The Greeks drained marshes there to make farmland. Epirus, Macedonia, and Thrace make up the regions of the northern Greek mainland.

Lots of Seas

Three seas surround Greece. The Ionian Sea is to the west. The Ionian Islands, including Corfu, lie there. In the far south is the Mediterranean Sea. The large island of Crete sits in this area.

The Ionian Sea washes the sandy shores of Corfu.

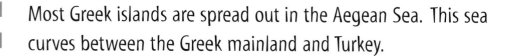

Most Greek islands are spread out in the Aegean Sea. This sea curves between the Greek mainland and Turkey.

Within the Aegean Sea are the Dodecanese, Sporades, and Cyclades Islands. Rhodes *(left)* is one of the main Dodecanese Islands.

It's Hot!

Greece has mostly mild weather. Winters can be rainy but are not too cold. Summers are quite hot.

A thirsty child grabs a drink on a hot summer day in Athens.

Greeks make sure they drink lots of water in the summer. They even rest in the late afternoon because of the heat.

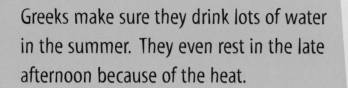

Nap Time!

Greece's hot summer weather has led to a local custom. Many Greeks enjoy siesta. This is a rest period in the afternoon between three and six. At this time, the weather is the hottest. During siesta, it's against the law to make loud noise!

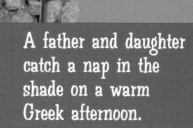

A father and daughter catch a nap in the shade on a warm Greek afternoon.

Getting from place to place can be tough when your home is surrounded by water!

Getting Around

Greece has about two thousand islands. How do people get from island to island? Or from the mainland to the islands?

Small boats, called ferries, take people around. Larger ferries dock at the country's major port cities.

Ferries carry people and cars to and from Greece's islands.

15

Long-Ago Greece

Greeks have been living on the mainland and the islands for thousands of years. Their civilization, or way of living, is one of the oldest in the world.

These old buildings in Athens offer a glimpse of Greece's early civilization.

The ancient Greeks built this temple in the town of Delphi.

Ancient Greeks believed in many gods. They built temples and named them after the gods. Ancient Greek gatherings, such as the Olympic Games, were set aside to honor the gods.

The First Olympics

The first Olympic Games were held in 776 B.C. This is more than 2,700 years ago! The ancient Greeks set up the games to honor Zeus, the king of the gods.

Becoming Greece

Greece has an old history. But at times, outsiders ruled the country. The last group of outsiders to rule Greece was the Ottoman Turks. They took over Greece in the 1400s. By the late 1700s, Greeks were working hard to win the right to rule themselves.

This Greek flag flies in Athens. Greece adopted the flag in 1822, after it won self-rule.

By 1821, Peloponnese and central Greece were free. The Ionian Islands joined modern Greece in 1864. Thessaly was added in 1881. Epirus, Macedonia, Thrace, and a bunch of islands came on board in the early 1900s. The Dodecanese joined in 1947.

Independence Day

Greece's regions won self-rule at different times. But all Greeks celebrate March 25 as Independence Day. On this day in 1821, the fight for self-rule began in northern Peloponnese.

Kids march in a parade celebrating Greek Independence Day.

Who Are the Greeks?

Modern Greeks take pride in their ancient culture. They are proud of being Greek and of speaking the Greek language. This language hasn't changed much since ancient times.

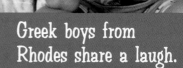

Greek boys from Rhodes share a laugh.

Small groups of Turks, Albanians, and Bulgarians also live in Greece. These groups often speak their own languages as well as Greek.

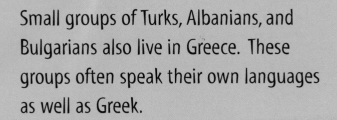

It's Greek to Me!

Greek's twenty-four-letter alphabet helped to shape the English alphabet. The first three Greek letters are alpha, beta, and gamma. These are much the same as the English letters *a*, *b*, and g.

Athens's sidewalks are busy with people. Almost all of them speak Greek!

Two girls enjoy the company of their grandmother.

A Package Deal

Greek families are large. And that's not because couples have lots of children. Typically, parents, grandparents, aunts, uncles, and cousins feel that they are part of one large group. They usually live near one another. Sometimes they live in the same building.

Greek family members eat together. They often cook and clean together. Kids have lots of playmates and babysitters. But it's tough to find time alone!

Children and their mother sit down together for lunch.

A Greek Church

Most Greeks belong to the Greek Orthodox Church. Easter is the most important Greek Orthodox holiday. Families gather for a big meal. It may include roast lamb, rice, and dill soup. Eggs are boiled and dyed red. Then they are baked in a loaf of bread.

Crack for Luck!

On Easter Sunday, the red eggs are taken out of the loaf. Each family member cracks his or her egg against another family member's egg. Greeks believe that luck will come to the person with the last uncracked egg.

Kids take part in an Easter service in a Greek Orthodox church.

Another major holiday is New Year's Day. It honors Saint Basil. Many Greeks believe that he grants wishes and brings gifts.

Greeks celebrate the New Year a little bit like other folks might celebrate Christmas. People give gifts. Families get together.

Fireworks explode over Athens on New Year's Eve.

City Life

Most Greeks live in cities. All the large cities are on the mainland.

A father and daughter fly a kite on a hill overlooking Athens.

26

Athens is the largest city in Greece. It is also the country's capital. Athens is named for the Greek goddess Athena.

Other large cities are Thessaloníki in northern Greece and Patras on Peloponnese.

Dear Aunt Mary,

We just came back from the Parthenon. It's awesome! The ancient Greeks built this temple to honor Athena. She's the Greek goddess of wisdom and war. The Parthenon sits high on a hill in Athens. I was sweating by the time I walked to the top!

See you soon!

A

The Parthenon

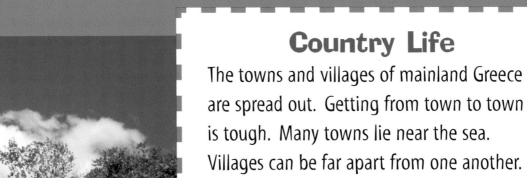

Country Life

The towns and villages of mainland Greece are spread out. Getting from town to town is tough. Many towns lie near the sea. Villages can be far apart from one another.

These kids live in a village outside of Athens.

Few people live in the northern mainland. But it's a wonderful area for wildlife. The Pindus Mountains cut off Epirus from the rest of Greece. This area is full of large animals and forested areas. Black bears, roe deer, and wild boars live there.

Bears walk through a forest in Greece's northern mainland.

Kids help fix fishing
nets on an island in
the Aegean Sea.

Island Life

Some Greek islands are popular vacation spots. Sandy beaches
and plenty of sun are common on these islands.

Other Greek islands don't draw as many travelers. Tourism isn't
so typical. Instead, people spend their time on these islands
fishing and doing other types of work.

Corfu, Crete, and Rhodes are all tourist islands. People travel to these islands year-round.

Some tourist islands close up in winter months. But Corfu, Crete, and Rhodes stay open all the time.

The islands of Corfu and Rhodes have special shows for tourists. Powerful music is played as lights flash off the islands' ancient ruins.

Growing Food

Greece's hot weather is excellent for growing food. Lemon trees, tomato plants, and grapes thrive. Thessaly is known for growing wheat. Oil from Greek olive trees is some of the world's best.

Olives grow on these trees in Peloponnese.

Sheep, goats, and other animals graze in the rocky pastures. Their milk is used as a drink and to make cheese. Feta is a goat cheese that's salty and crumbly. It is eaten by itself or in salads or soups.

Let's Eat!

The evening meal in Greece is a time for family and friends to visit. They share news over olives, feta cheese, and tomatoes. Main courses usually include meat and rice. Dolmas, for example, are grape leaves stuffed with rice and ground meat. Spanakopita is spinach, onions, and cheese in a light, flaky crust.

Traditional Greek foods, including dolmas *(top left)* and olives *(bottom right)* make a delicious meal.

Baklava is a sweet and tasty treat.

Have a Look!

At a Greek restaurant, owners expect guests to go in the kitchen. They want customers to have a look at what's cooking! Diners can ask questions. They can watch as cooks prepare the dishes.

Greeks also enjoy local seafoods. These might include octopus, lobster, squid, and shrimp. Honey is used as a sweetener in Greek desserts. Baklava is pastry with layers of honey and nuts. Yum!

Come and Visit!

Many people visit Greece during spring and summer. They may hop from island to island or stay in one place.

Visitors enjoy the warm, sandy beaches on Greek islands.

A tourist shops at a street market in Greece.

Tourists may lie on a beach or visit the many ancient ruins throughout the country. They may shop until they drop!

Greek Dancing

Traditional dancing is still learned and performed throughout Greece. Two types are popular. One dance style involves leaping. The other has dancers shuffling in a line or circle.

Young girls in costume perform a traditional Greek dance.

Typically, men and boys dance separately from women and girls. The Dora Stratou troupe holds concerts every summer in Athens to treat tourists to traditional Greek dances.

39

These boys show off their dancing skills onstage.

School

Greek kids start school at the age of six. They take six years of basic classes to learn reading, math, and other skills. After that, they take three years of harder classes.

A teacher works with kids in his classroom.

Greek students can leave school at the age of fifteen. But a lot of kids choose to stay in school. Some may move on to college.

Greek students work hard to learn their lessons.

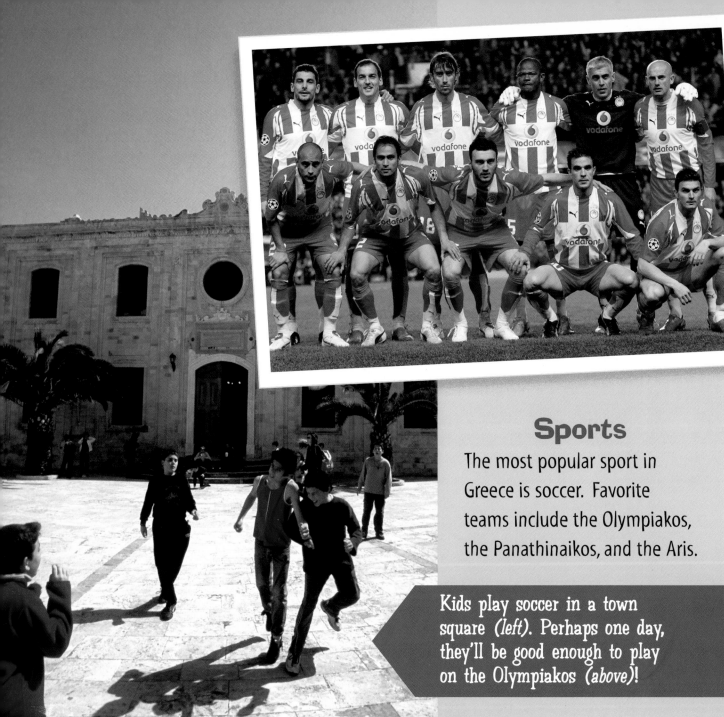

Sports

The most popular sport in Greece is soccer. Favorite teams include the Olympiakos, the Panathinaikos, and the Aris.

Kids play soccer in a town square *(left)*. Perhaps one day, they'll be good enough to play on the Olympiakos *(above)*!

Basketball is also becoming a huge sport in Greece. Guess what? Several of the basketball team names are the same as in soccer!

The Olympic Games—Ancient and Modern

The last ancient Olympics were held in A.D. 393. The first modern Olympics took place about 1,600 years later in 1896. They were in Athens. Summer sports—such as wrestling, track, and swimming—were on the program. A Greek runner named Spiridon Louis thrilled Greek fans by winning the gold medal for the marathon race.

A Panathinaikos player (in white) tries to block the shot of an Olympiakos athelete (red).

THE FLAG OF GREECE

Greece's flag is blue and white. These colors make people think of the bright blue sky and the white sea waves that surround the country. A cross is in the top left-hand corner. It stands for the honor Greek people have for the Greek Orthodox Church.

FAST FACTS

FULL COUNTRY NAME: Hellenic Republic

AREA: 50,961 square miles (131,988 square kilometers), or slightly smaller than the state of Alabama

MAIN LANDFORMS: the Pindus Mountains; the regions Epirus, Euboea, Attica, Boeotia, Macedonia, Thessaly, and Thrace; the peninsula called the Peloponnese; the Ionian Islands, Cyclades Islands, Dodecanese Islands, and Sporades Islands

MAJOR RIVERS: Achelous, Peneus, Vardar

ANIMALS AND THEIR HABITATS: black bears, roe deer, wolves (Epirus); chamois (northern Greece); ibex (Crete); sea lions, pelicans (Aegean Sea); nightingales (mainland Greece)

CAPITAL CITY: Athens

OFFICIAL LANGUAGE: Greek

POPULATION: about 11.2 million

GLOSSARY

ancient: very old

civilization: the way of life of a people, including their accomplishments in art and science

continent: any one of seven large areas of land. The continents are Africa, Antarctica, Asia, Australia, Europe, North America, and South America.

culture: the way of life, ideas, and customs of a particular group of people

ferry: a small boat used to carry goods and people

Hellas: another name for Greece

island: a piece of land surrounded by water

mainland: the main part of a country, separate from its islands

map: a drawing or chart of all or part of Earth or the sky

mountain: a part of Earth's surface that rises high into the sky

peninsula: a piece of land that has water on three sides

port: a place on the water where boats can dock

temple: a place of worship

tourism: the practice of traveling for enjoyment or pleasure

tourist: a person who travels for enjoyment or pleasure, or a place that attracts such a person

TO LEARN MORE

BOOKS

Haskins, Jim, and Kathleen Benson. *Count Your Way through Greece.* Minneapolis: Millbrook Press, 1996. Get to know Greece and its language through the numbers one through ten. Each number is linked to something important about Greece.

Ryan, Patrick. *Greece.* Chanhassen, MN: Child's World, 2003. Learn more about the people and places of Greece in this book.

Storrie, Paul. *Hercules: The Twelve Labors.* Minneapolis: Graphic Universe, 2007. This graphic novel tells the story of the superhuman hero of ancient Greece.

Waryncia, Lou. *If I Were a Kid in Ancient Greece.* Peterborough, NH: Cricket Books, 2006. This book shows what life was like for children in ancient Greece.

Weber, Belinda. *The Best Book of Ancient Greece.* New York: Kingfisher, 2005. Discover what are the coolest things about ancient Greece in this colorful book.

WEBSITES

Enchanted Learning
http://www.enchantedlearning.com/geography
This site has pages to label and color of Greece and its flag.

Time for Kids
http://www.timeforkids.com/TFK/teachers/aw/wr/main/0,28132,588097,00.html
This site on Greece includes a quiz, pictures, and a timeline.

INDEX

The images in this book are used with the permission of: © Hemis.fr/SuperStock, pp. 4, 10; © age fotostock/SuperStock, pp. 6, 16, 17, 32; © Jon Arnold Images/SuperStock, p. 7; © Sotirios Milionis/Alamy, p. 8; © Martin Gray/National Geographic/Getty Images, p. 9; © Colin Paterson/SuperStock, p. 11; © Louisa Gouliamaki/AFP/Getty Images, p. 12; © Steve Bentley/Alamy, p. 13; © Bob Turner/Art Directors & TRIP, p. 14; © Helene Rogers/Art Directors & TRIP, pp. 15, 18; © Robert Harding Picture Library Ltd/Alamy, p. 19; © WoodyStock/Alamy, p. 20; © Richard Nowitz/National Geographic/Getty Images, p. 21; © Heimo Aga/drr.net, p. 22; © Clairy Moustafellou/IML Image Group/drr.net, pp. 23, 28; © Velissarios Voutsas/IML Image Group/drr.net, p. 24; © Aris Messinis/AFP/Getty Images, p. 25; © Anna Watson/Axiom Photographic Agency/Getty Images, p. 26; © Natalia Pavlova/Dreamstime.com, p. 27; © IML Image Group Ltd/Alamy, pp. 29, 30, 42 (left); © Chris Lock, p. 31; © Peter Horree/Alamy, p. 33; © Simon Reddy/Alamy, p. 34; © foodfolio/Alamy, p. 35; © Sean Gallup/Getty Images, p. 36; © Colin Paterson/Photodisc/Getty Images, p. 37; © Nikos Desyllas/SuperStock, p. 38; © sami moudavaris/Alamy, p. 39; © Owen Franken/CORBIS, pp. 40, 41; © Jamie McDonald/Getty Images, p. 42 (top); AP Photo/Thanassis Stavrakis, p. 43. Illustrations by © Bill Hauser/Independent Picture Service.
Front Cover: © Jon Arnold Images Ltd/Alamy.